Copyright © 2018 Skye Wright

All rights reserved.

Title ID: 8252674
ISBN-13: 978-1986573788
ISBN-10: 1986573788

Birds Eye View

A Coloring Book by Skye Wright

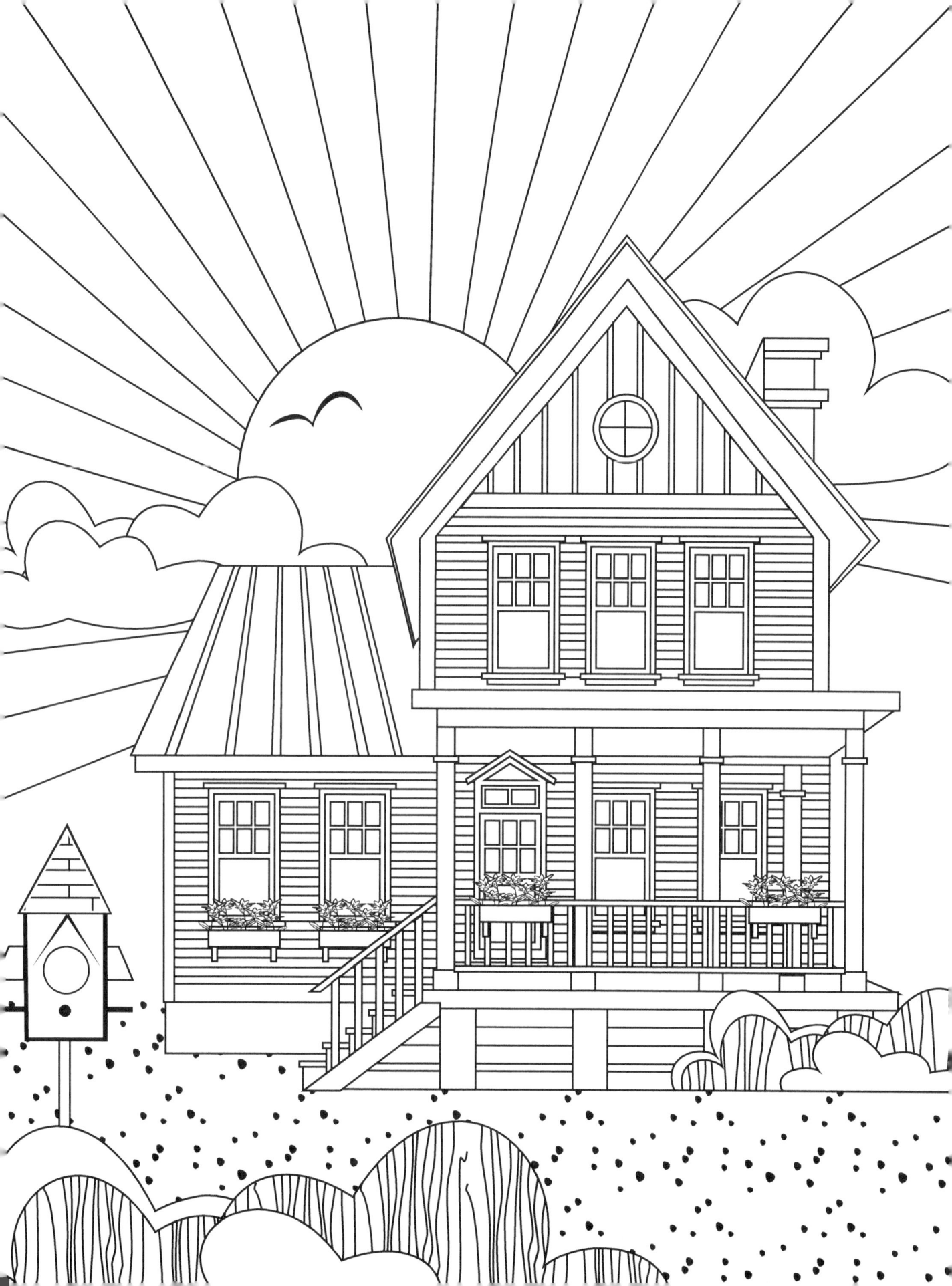

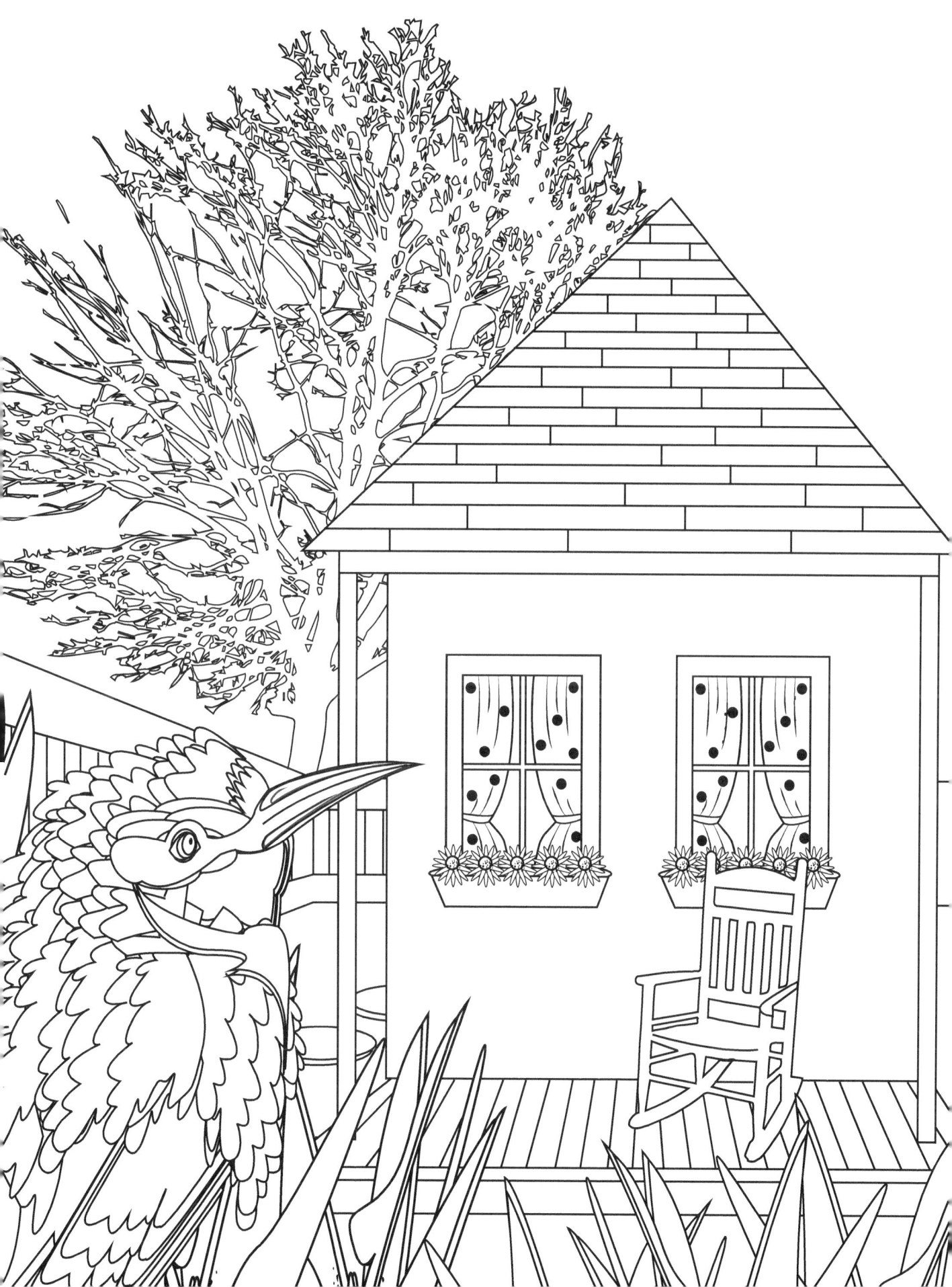

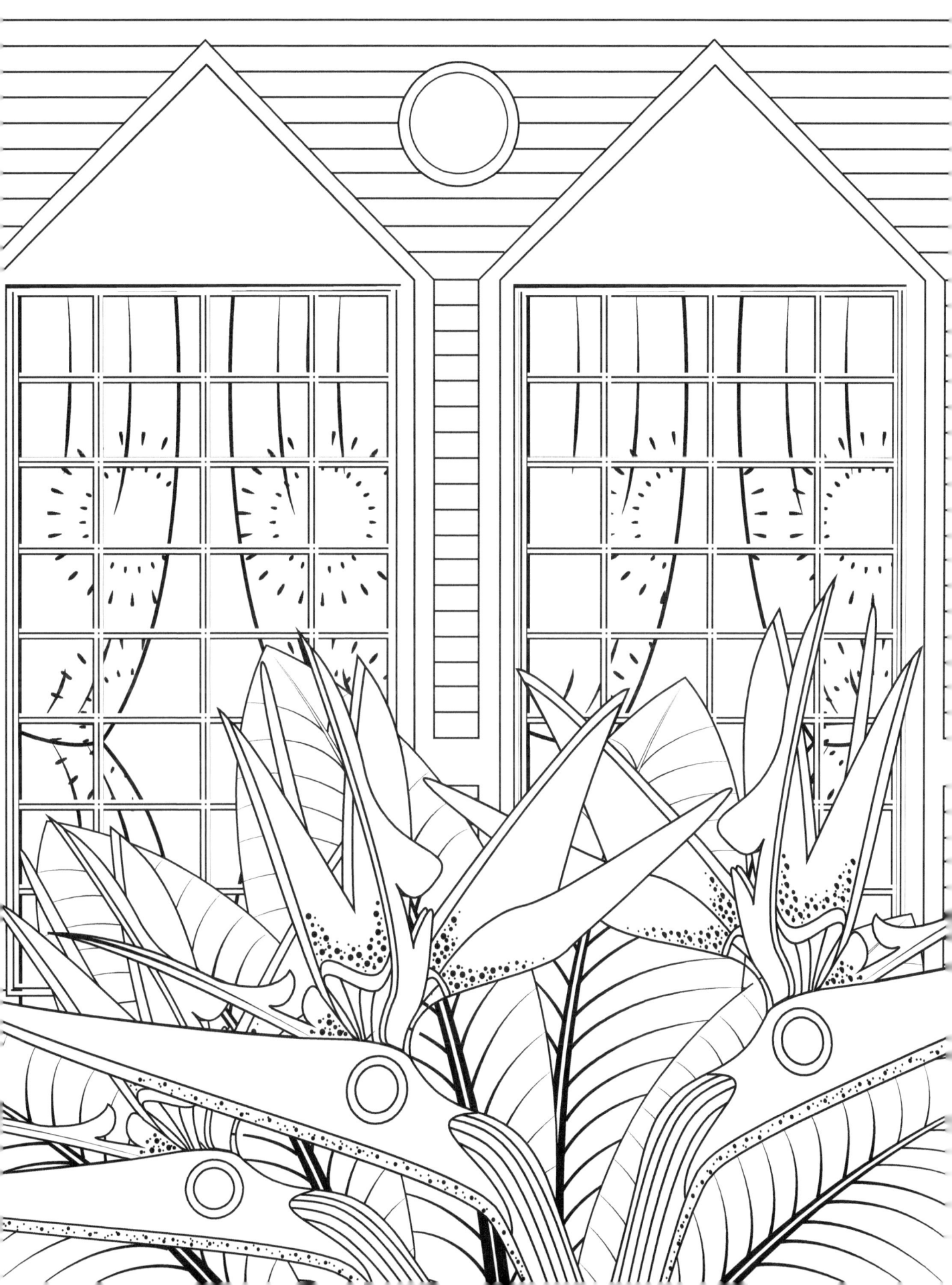

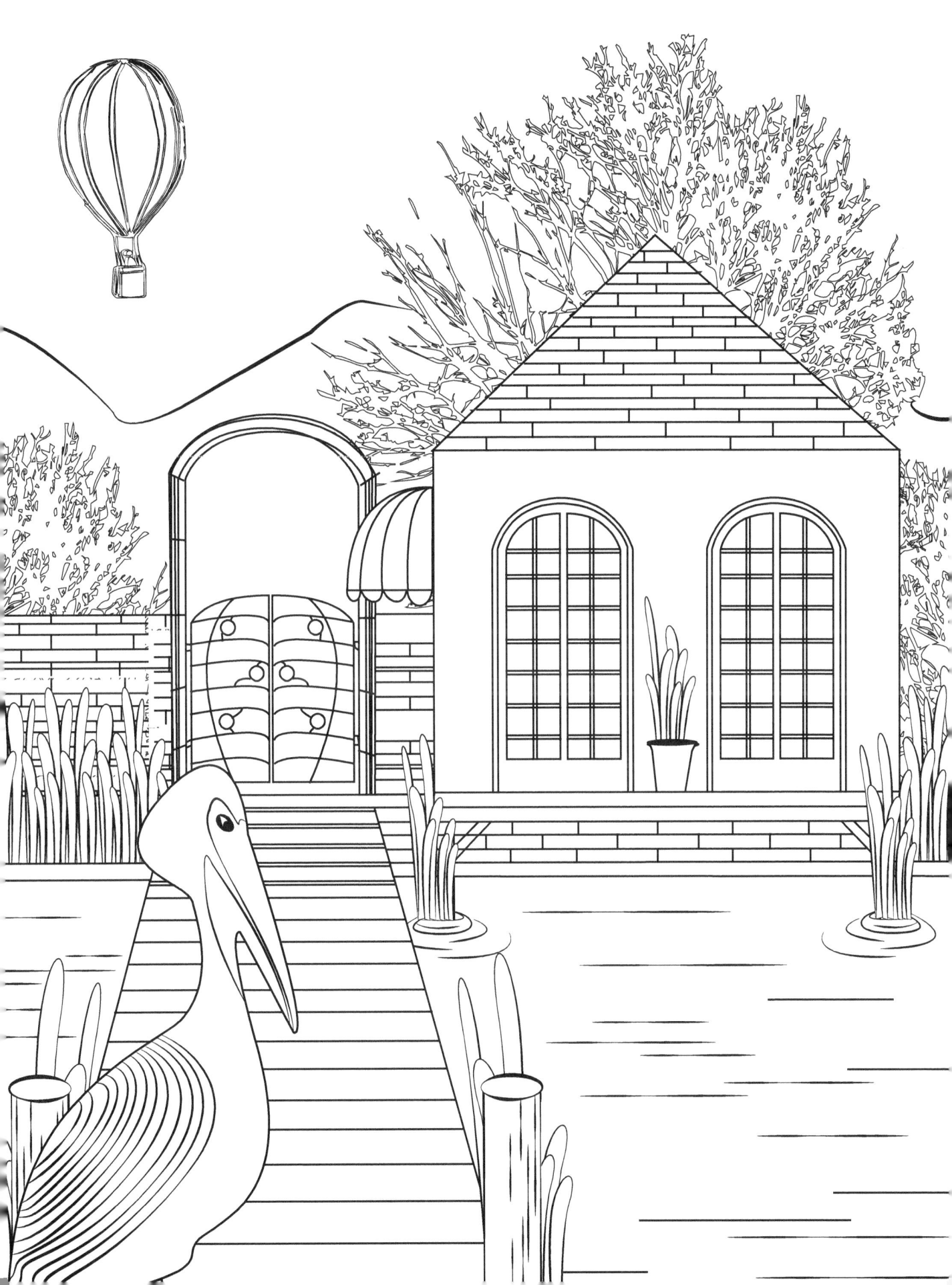

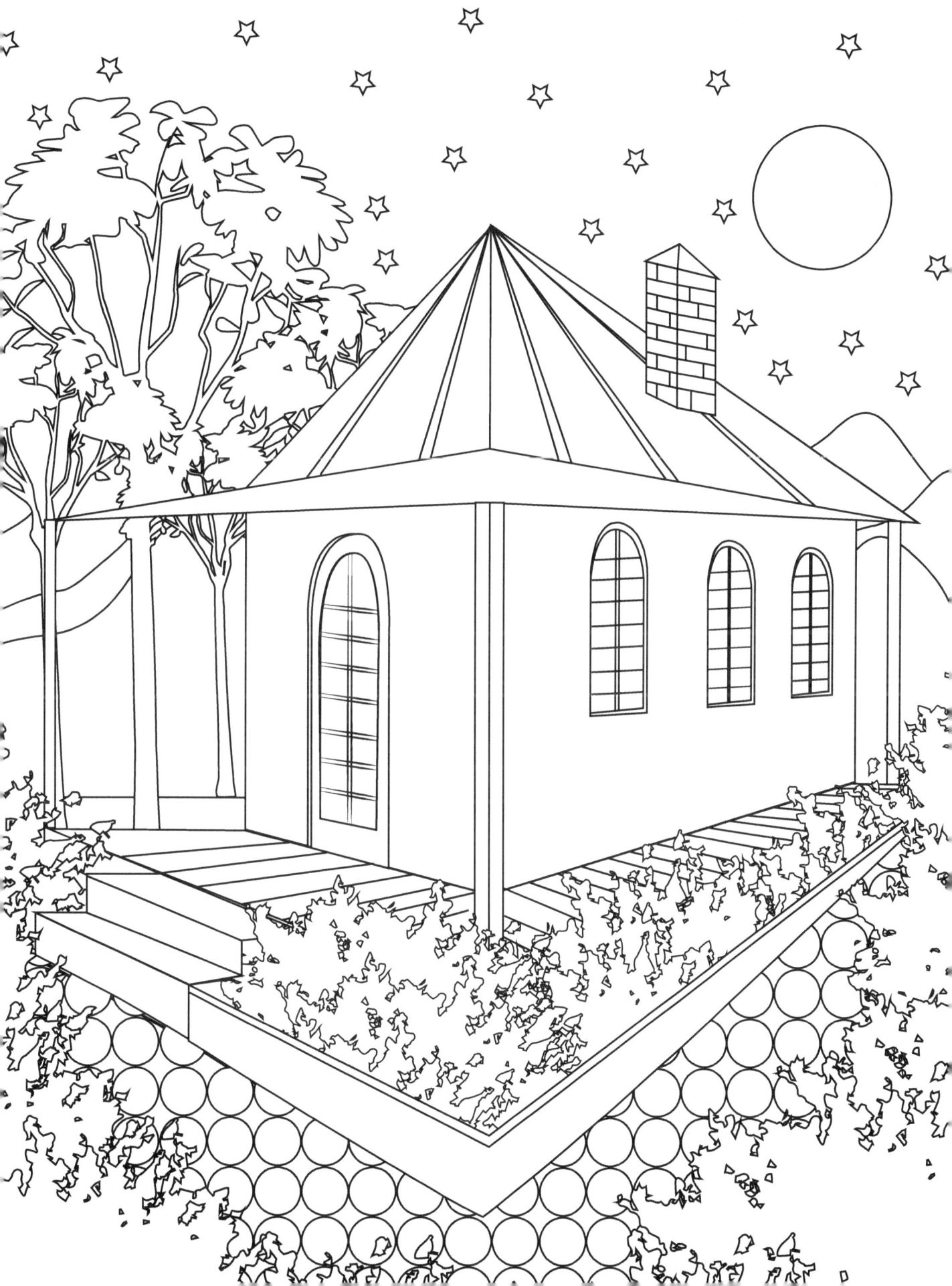

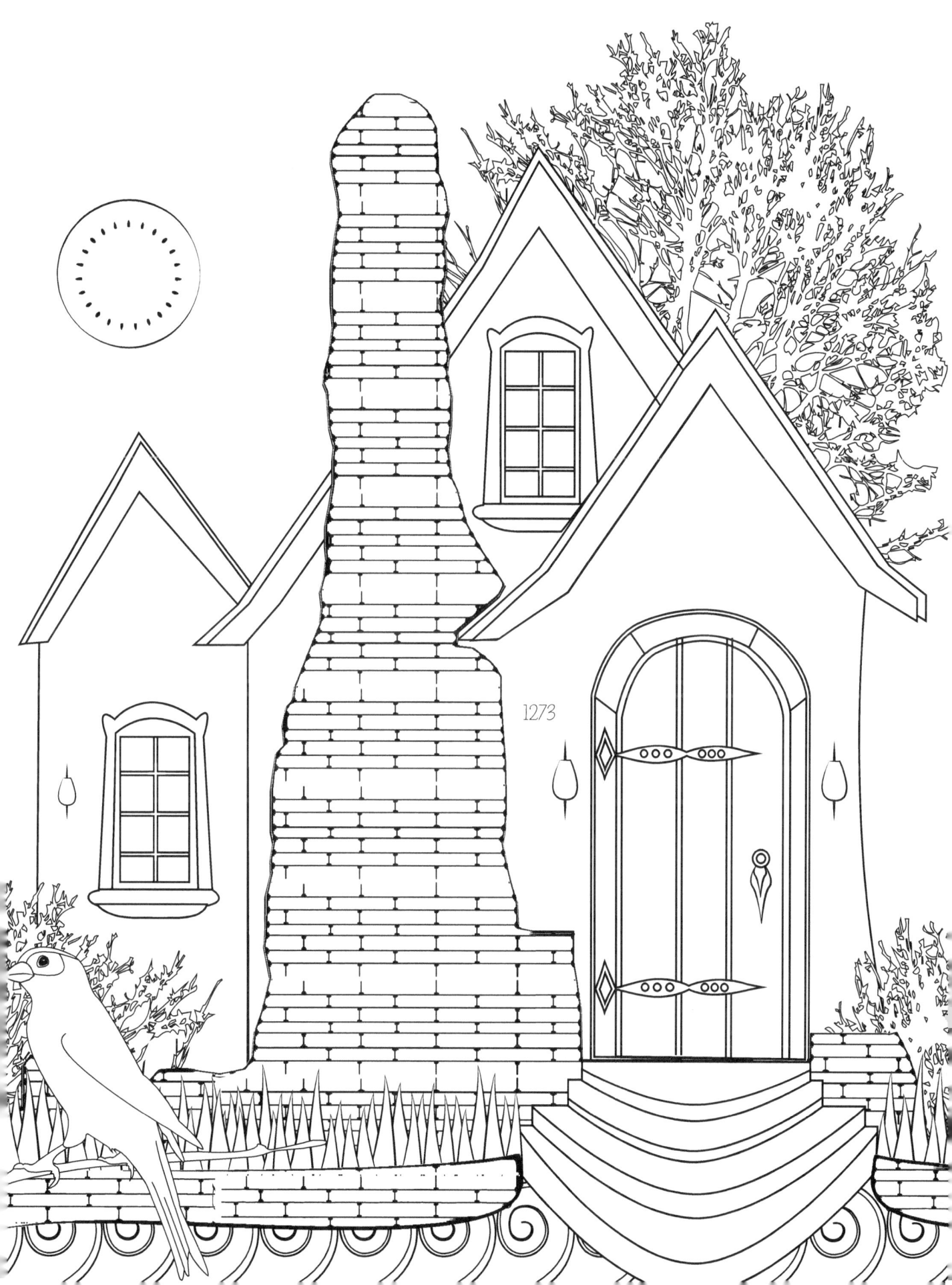

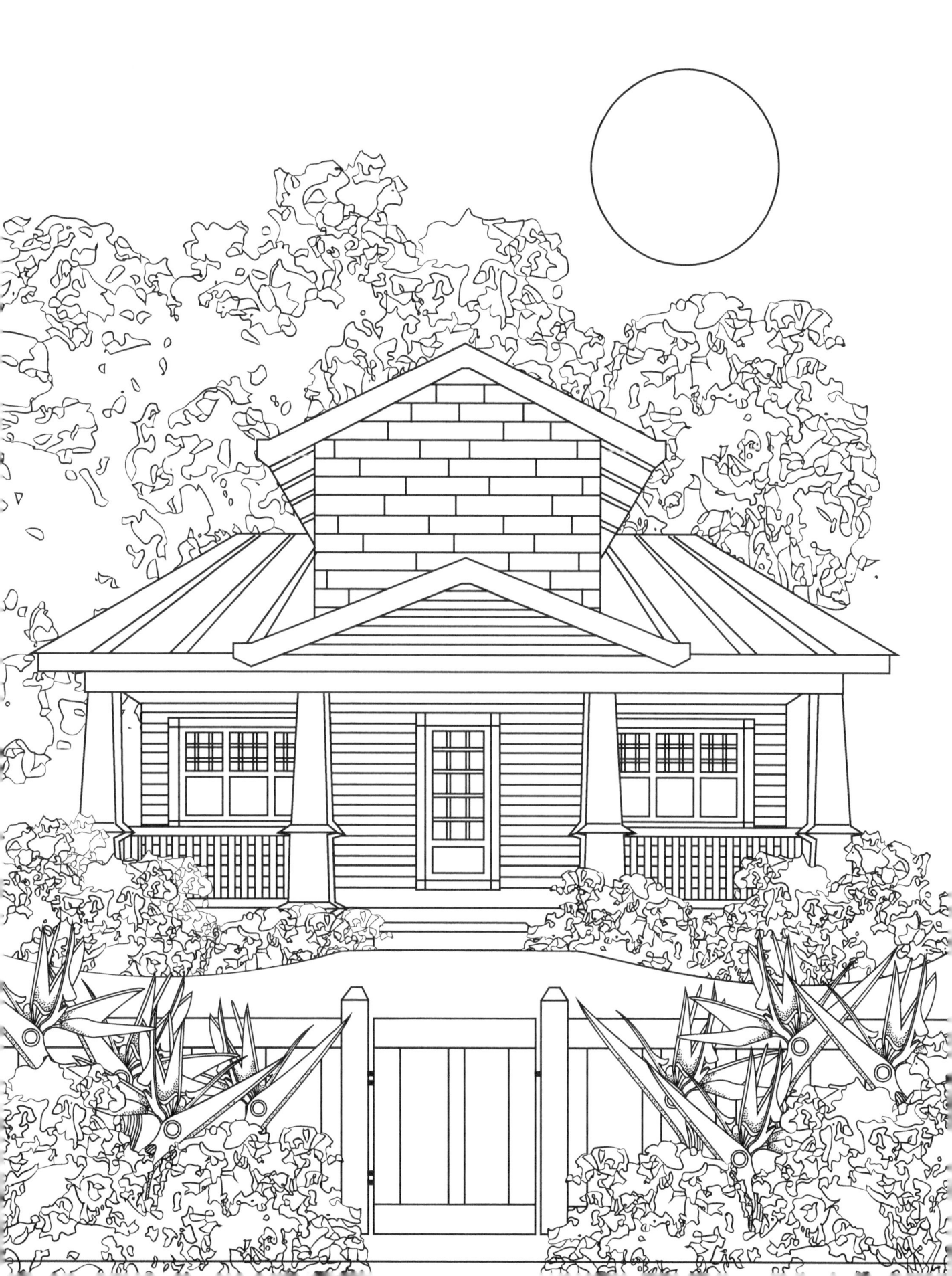

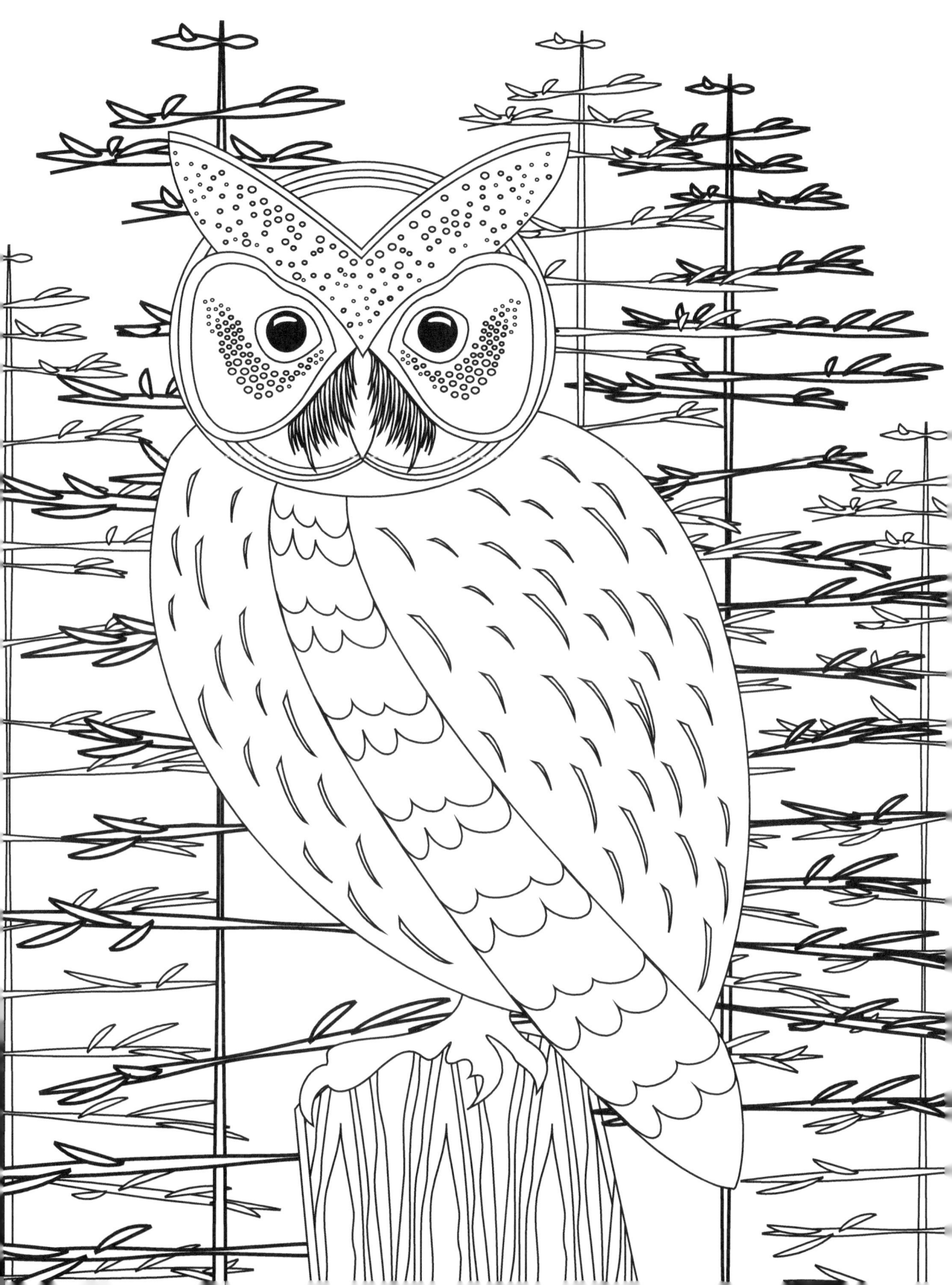

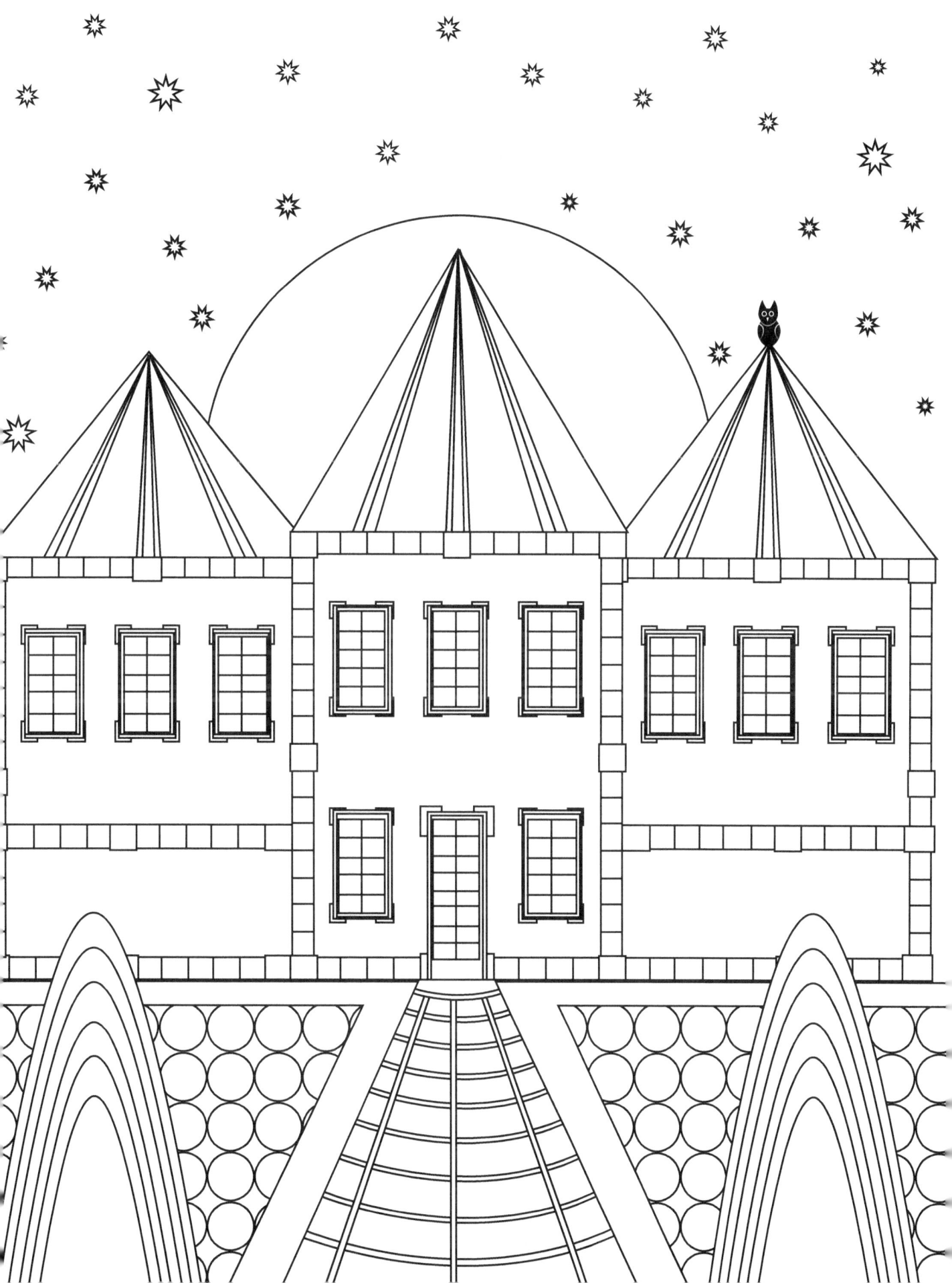

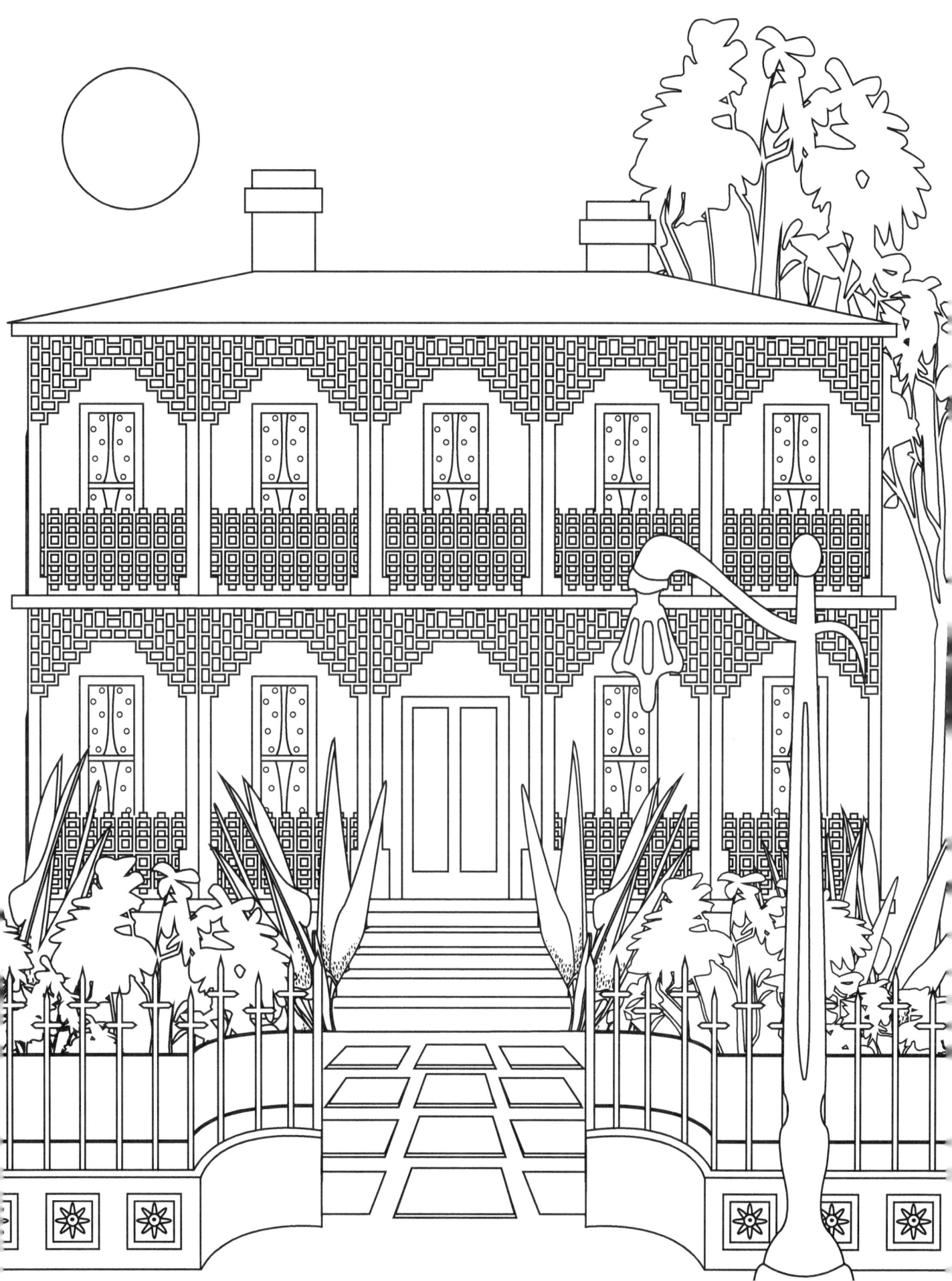

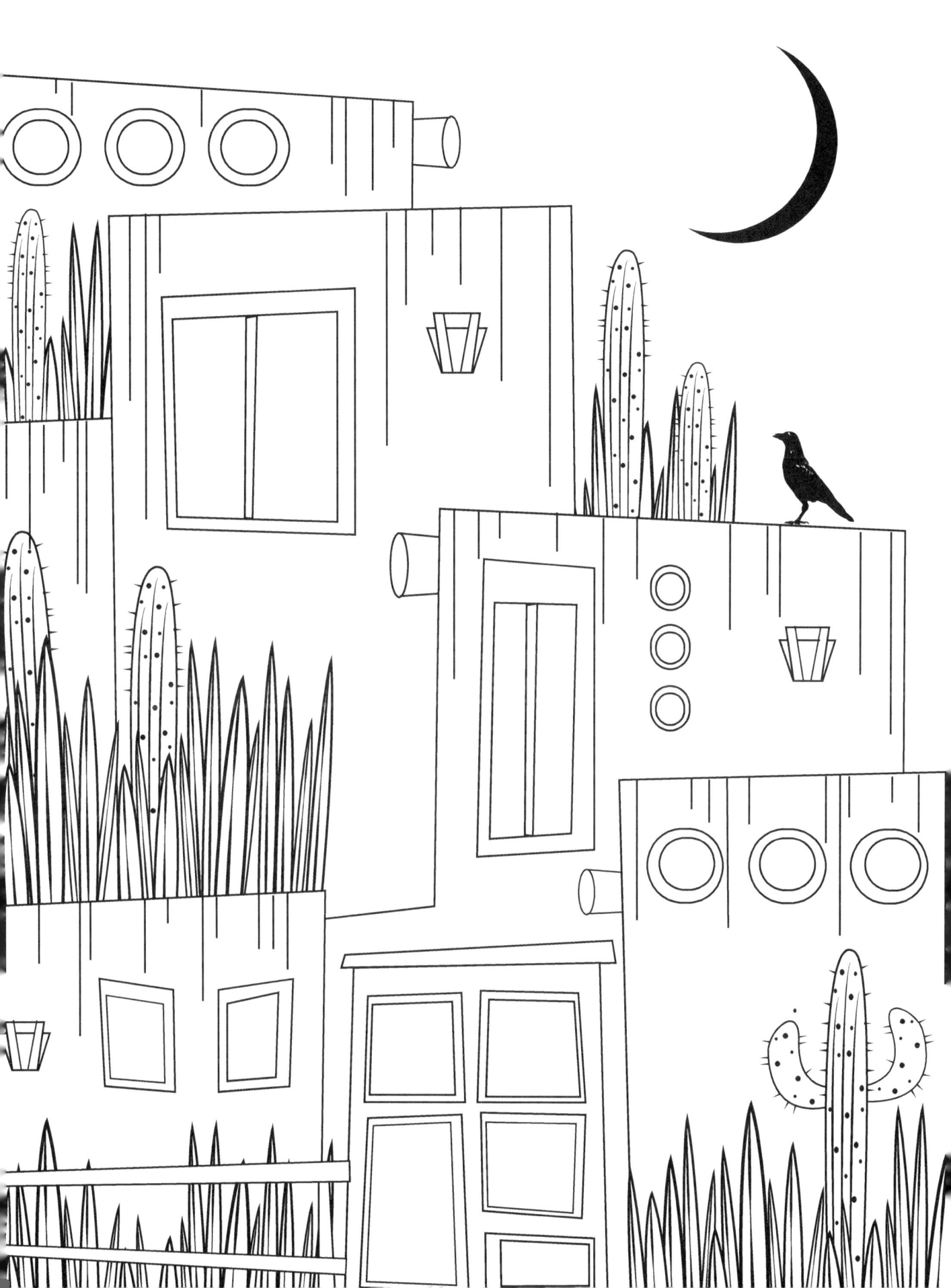

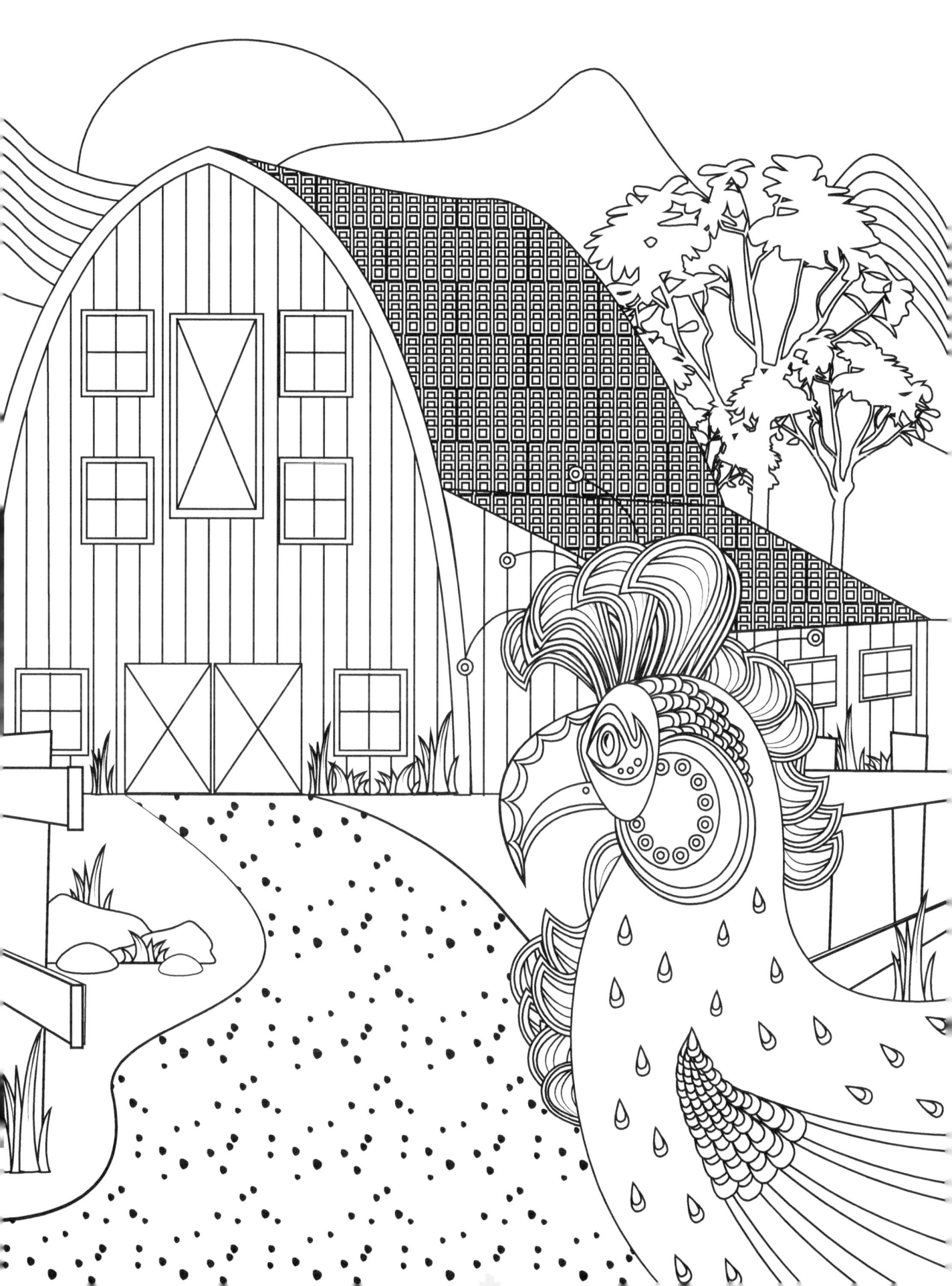

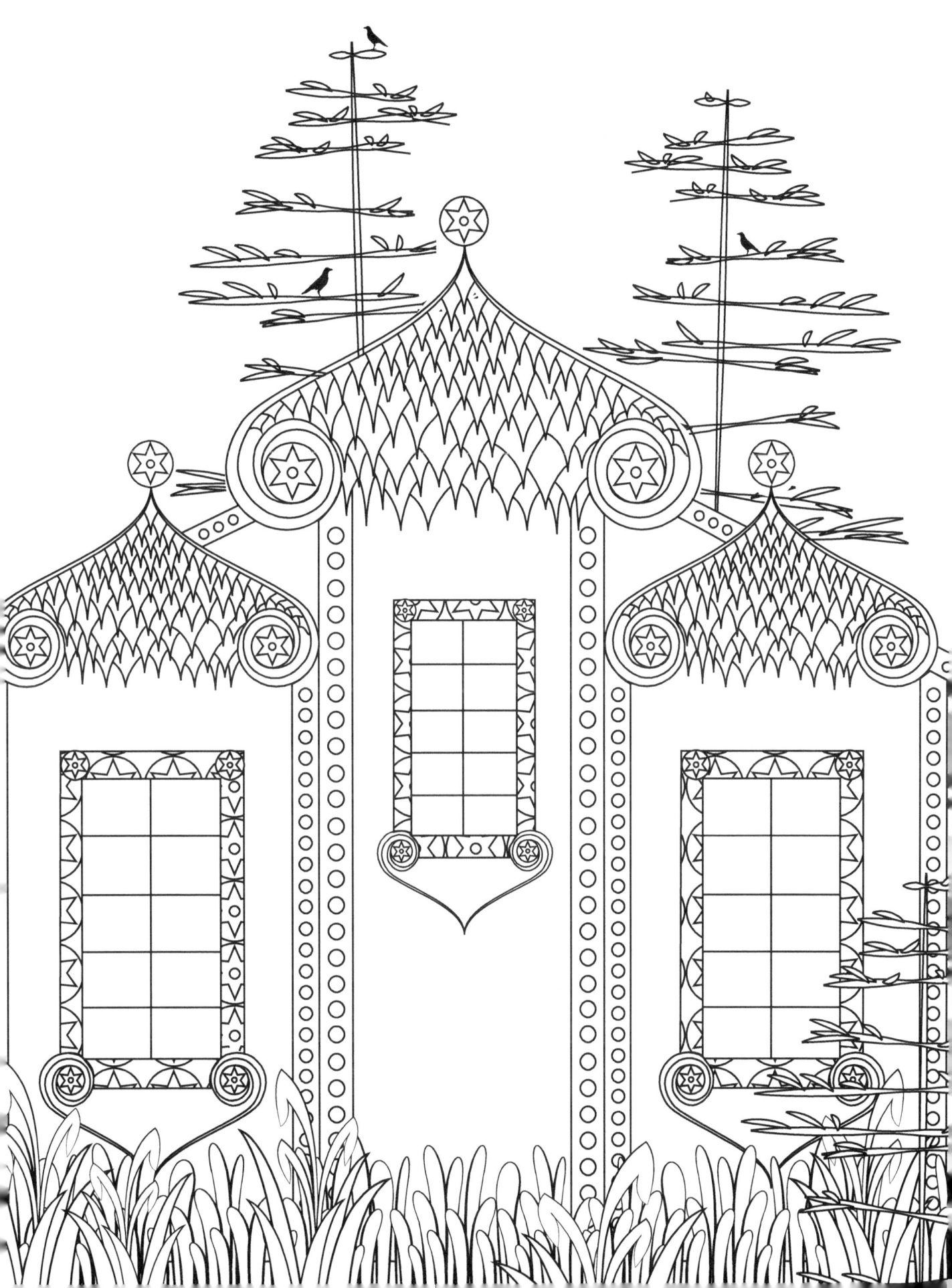

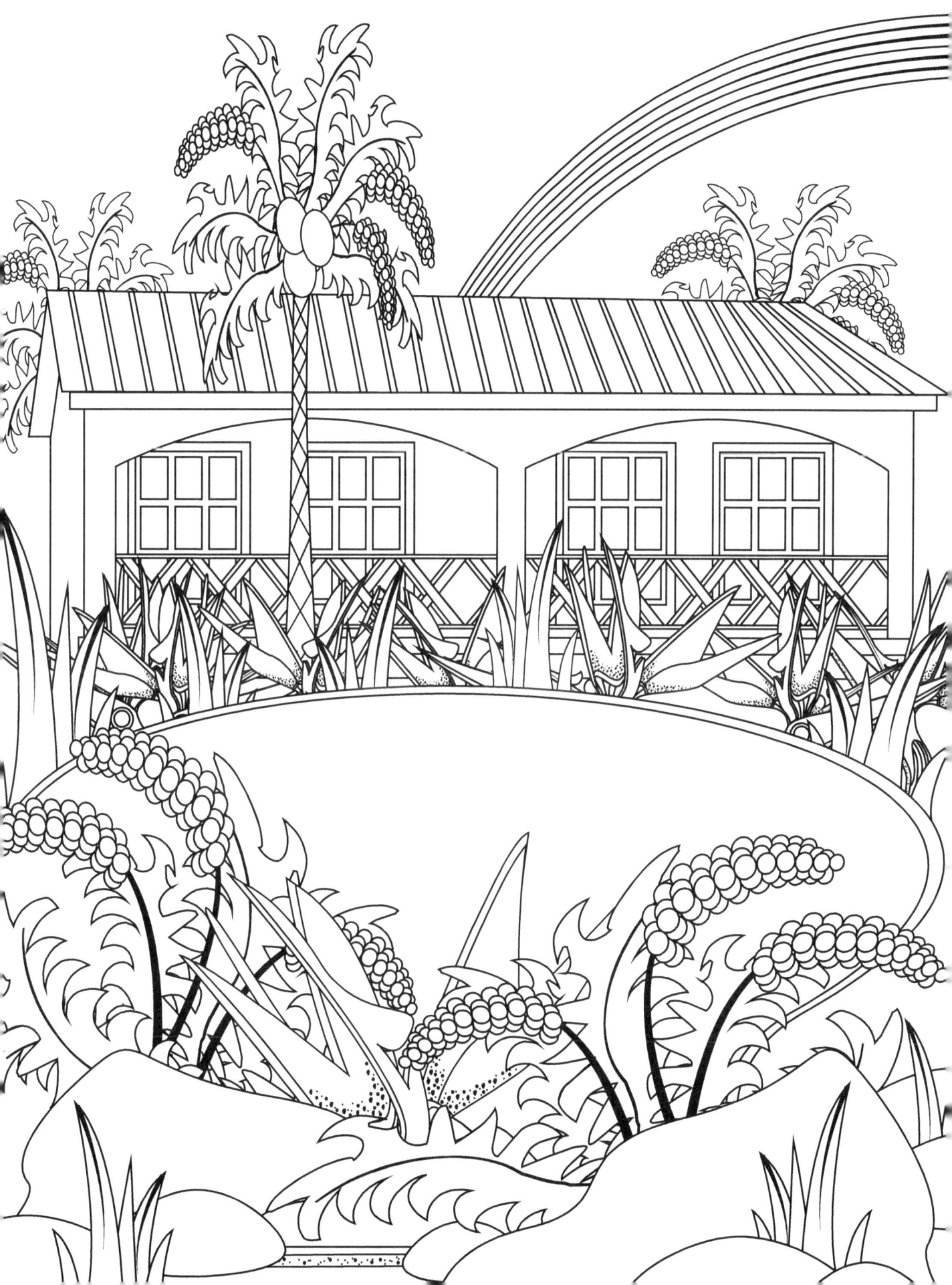

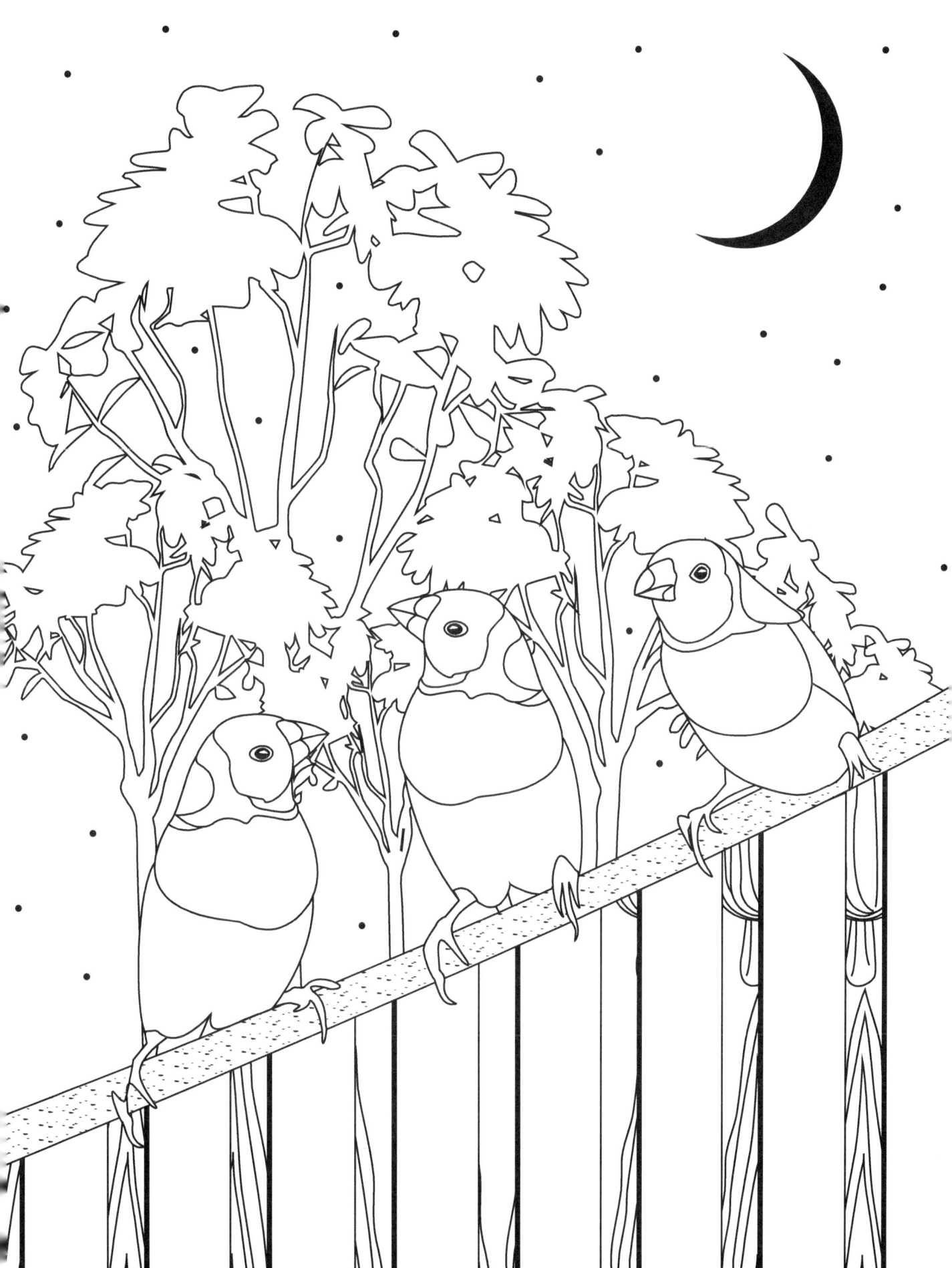

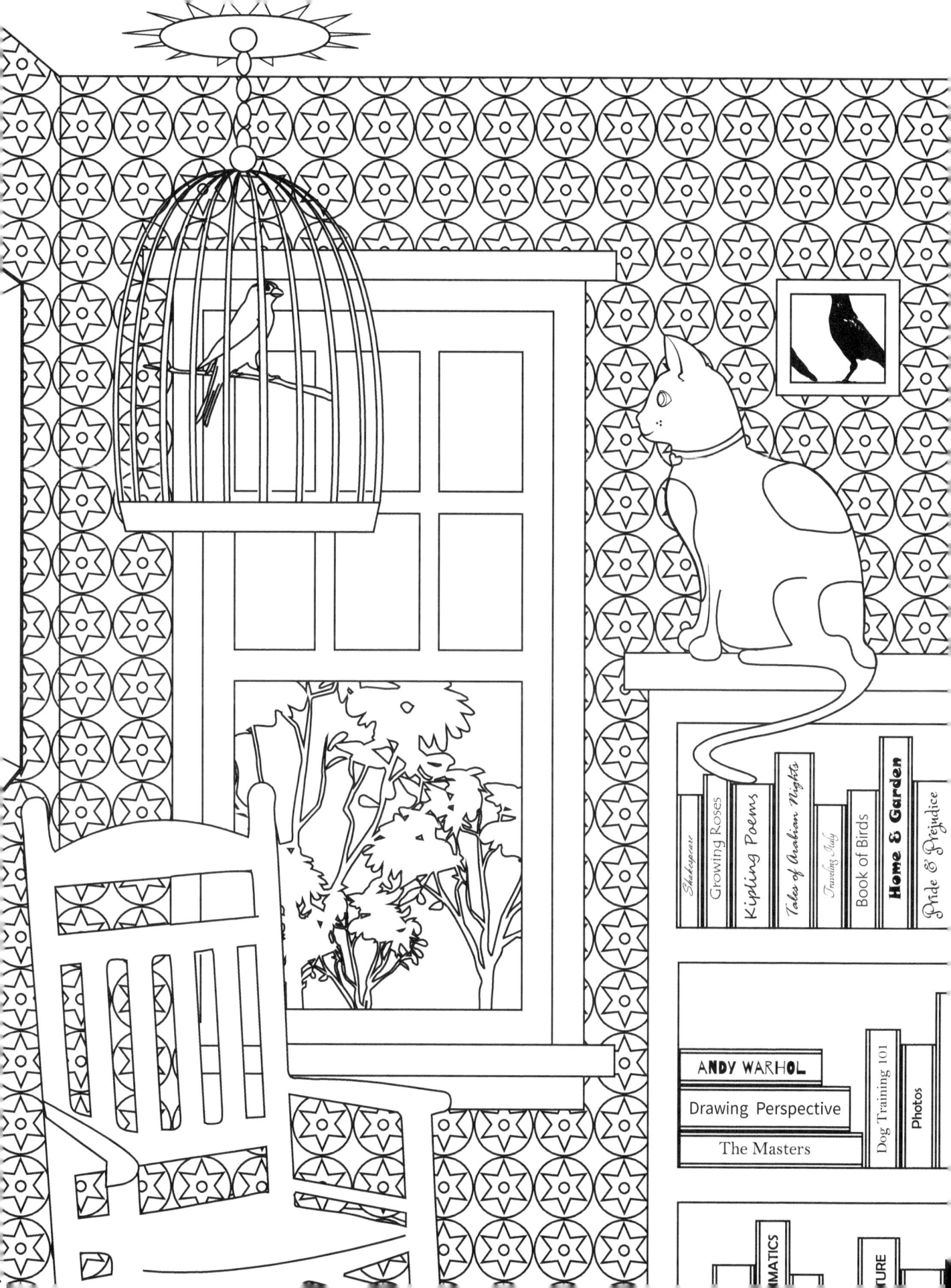

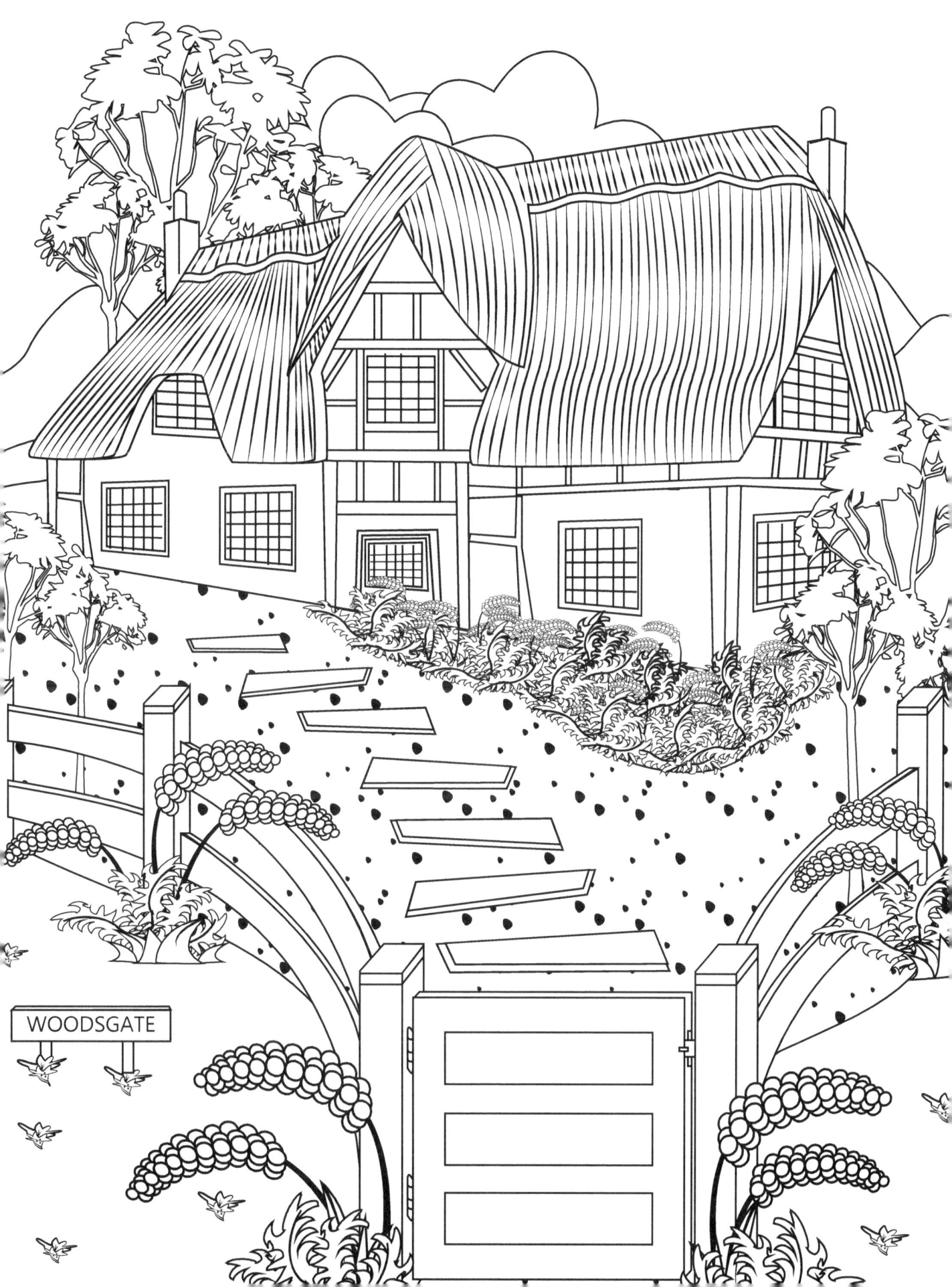

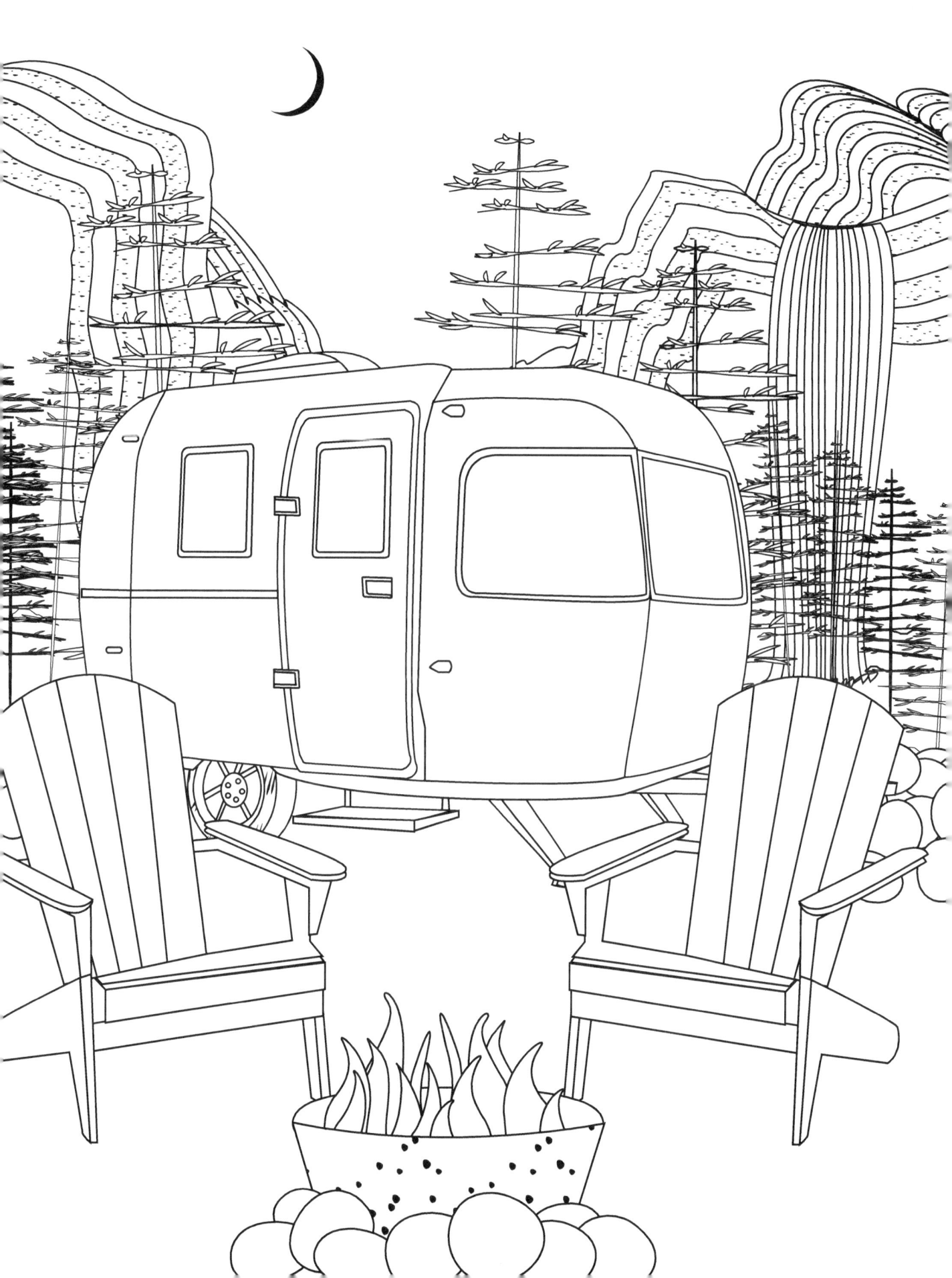

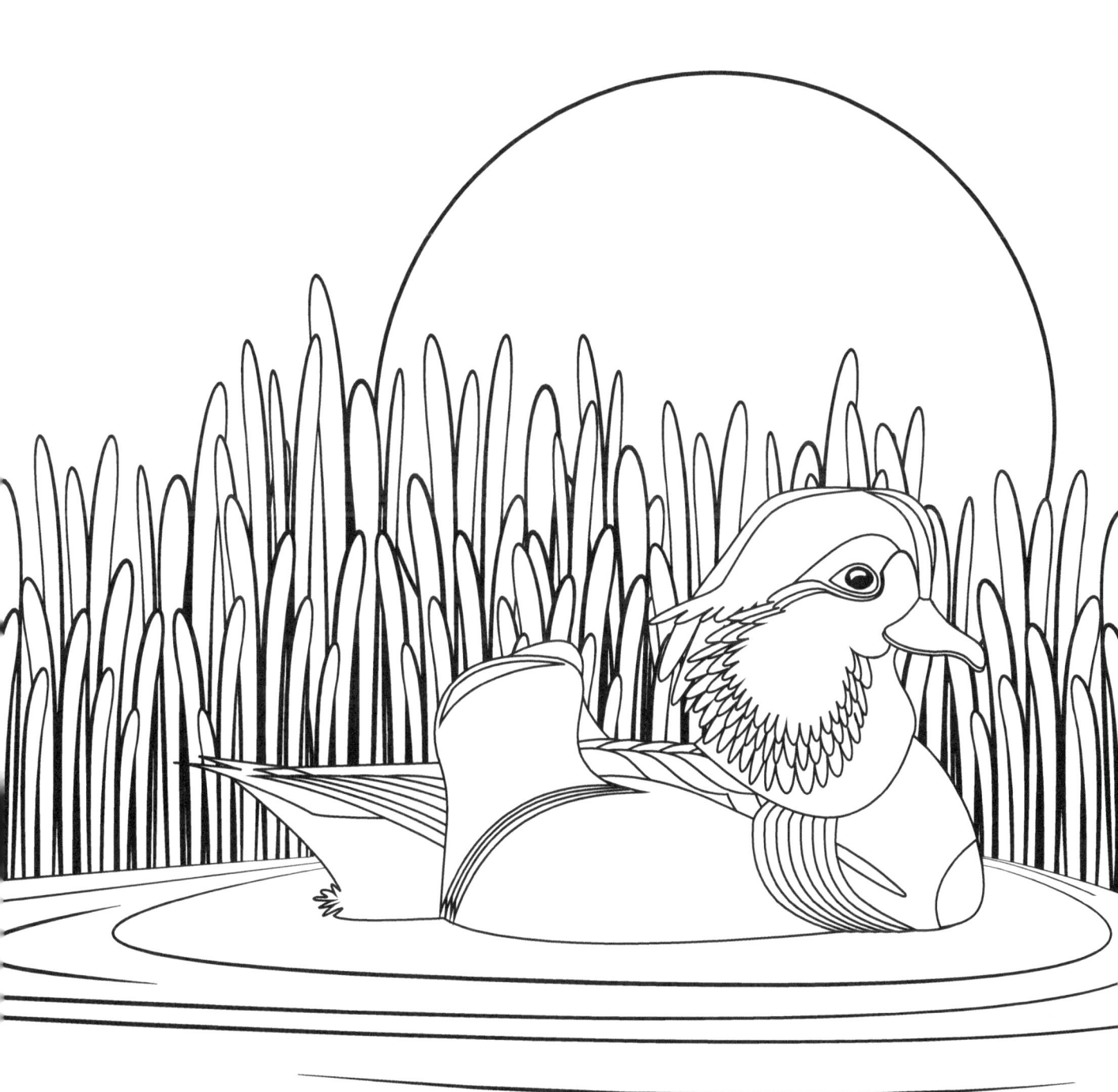

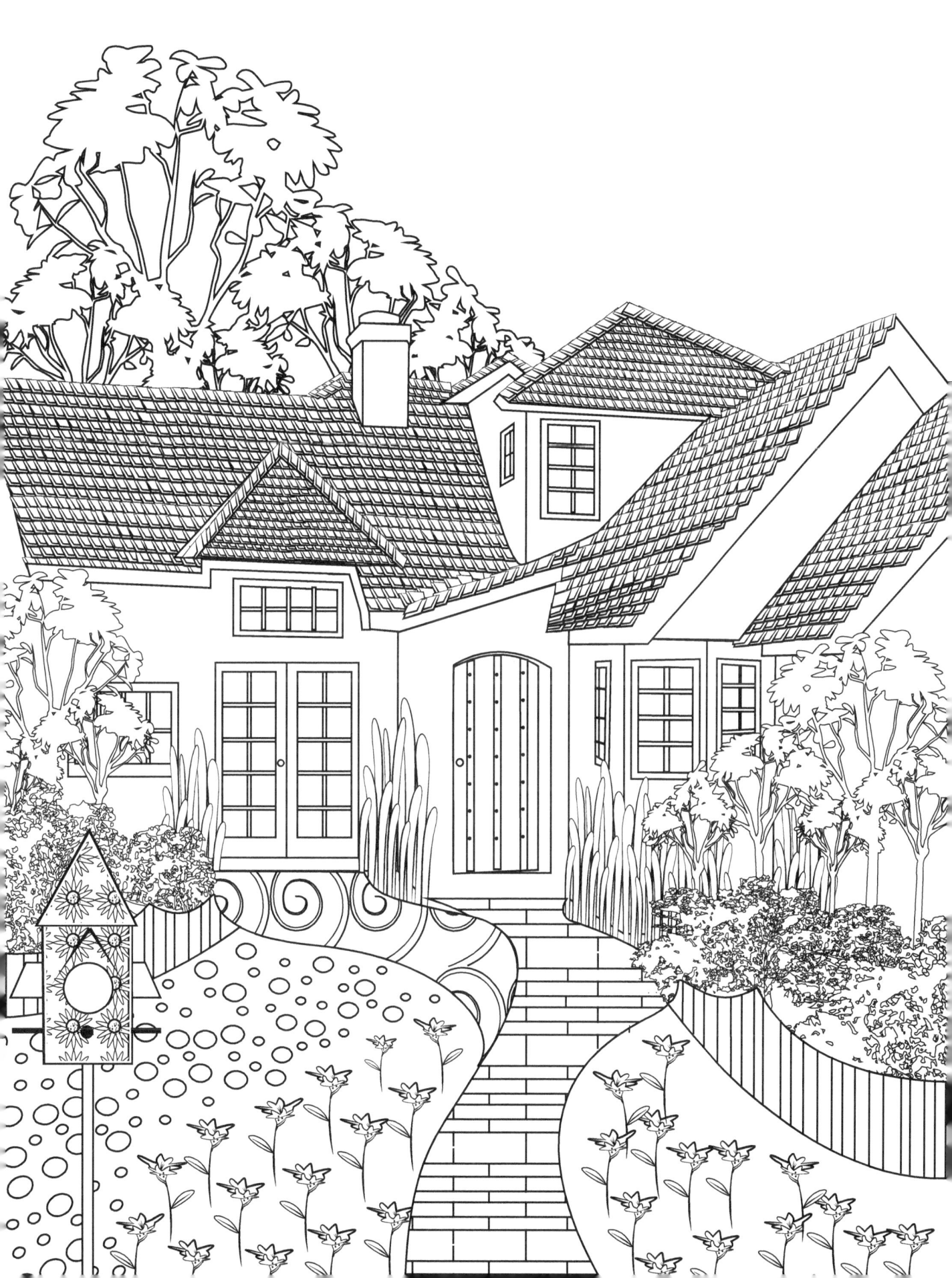

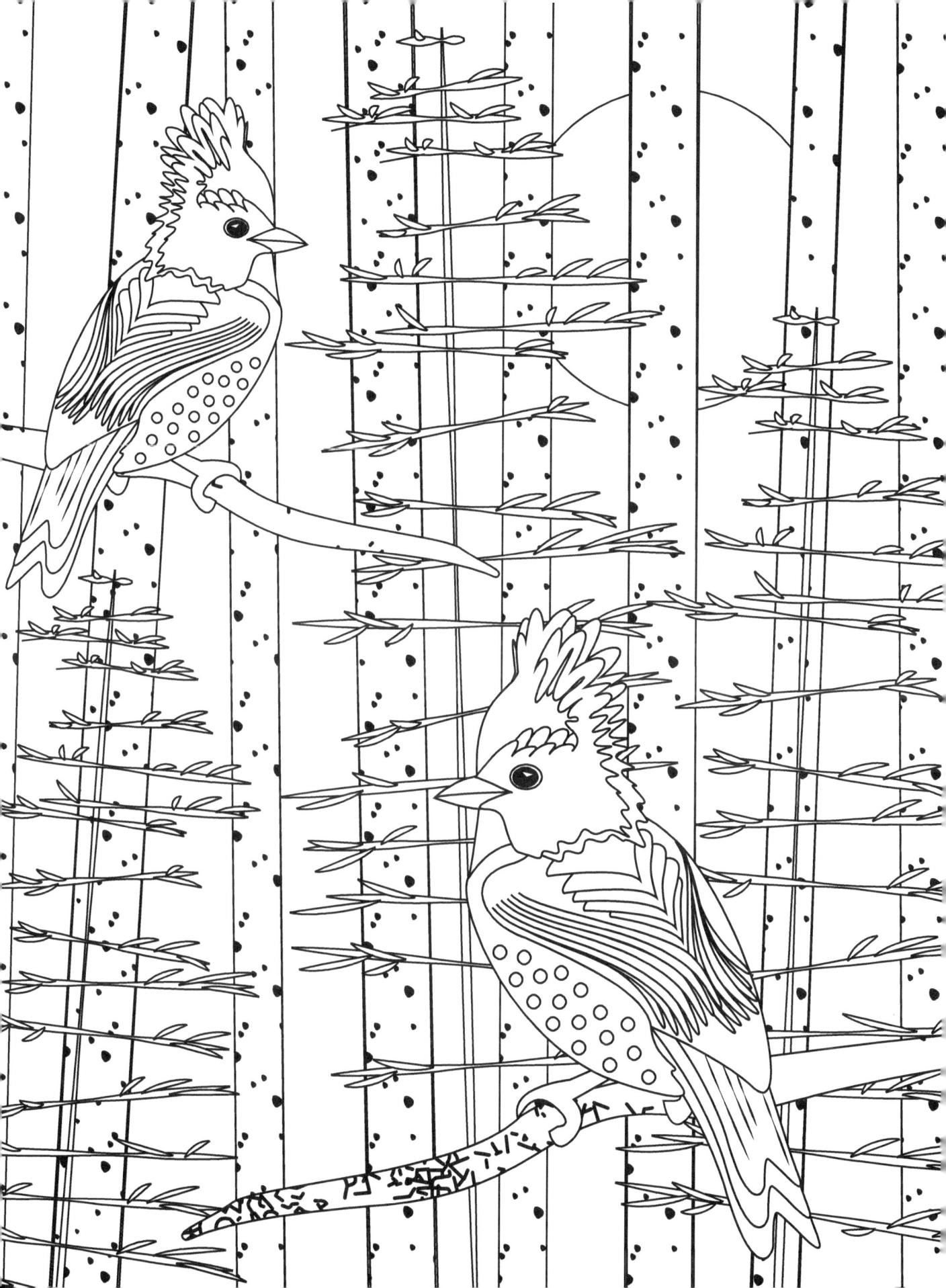

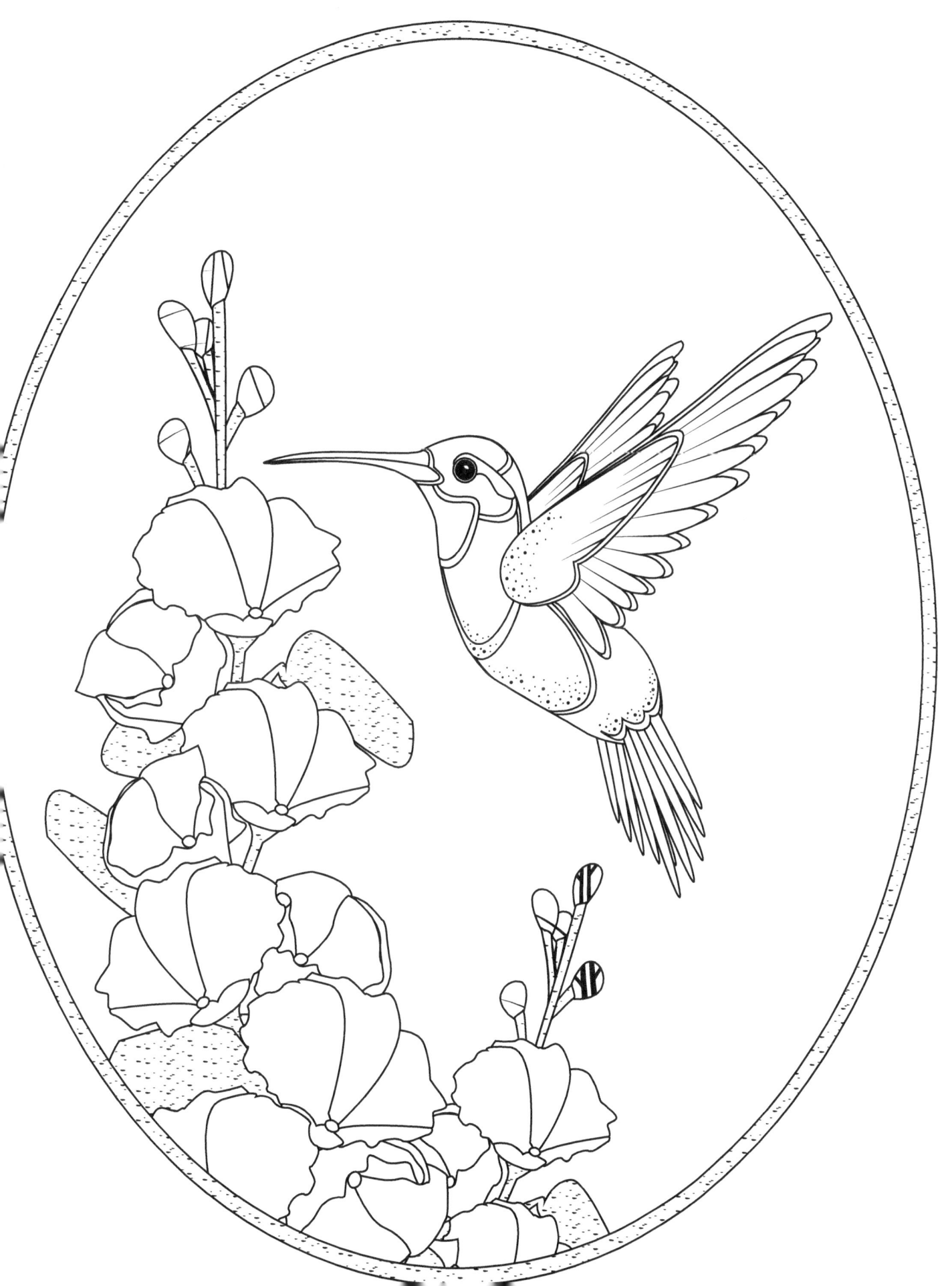

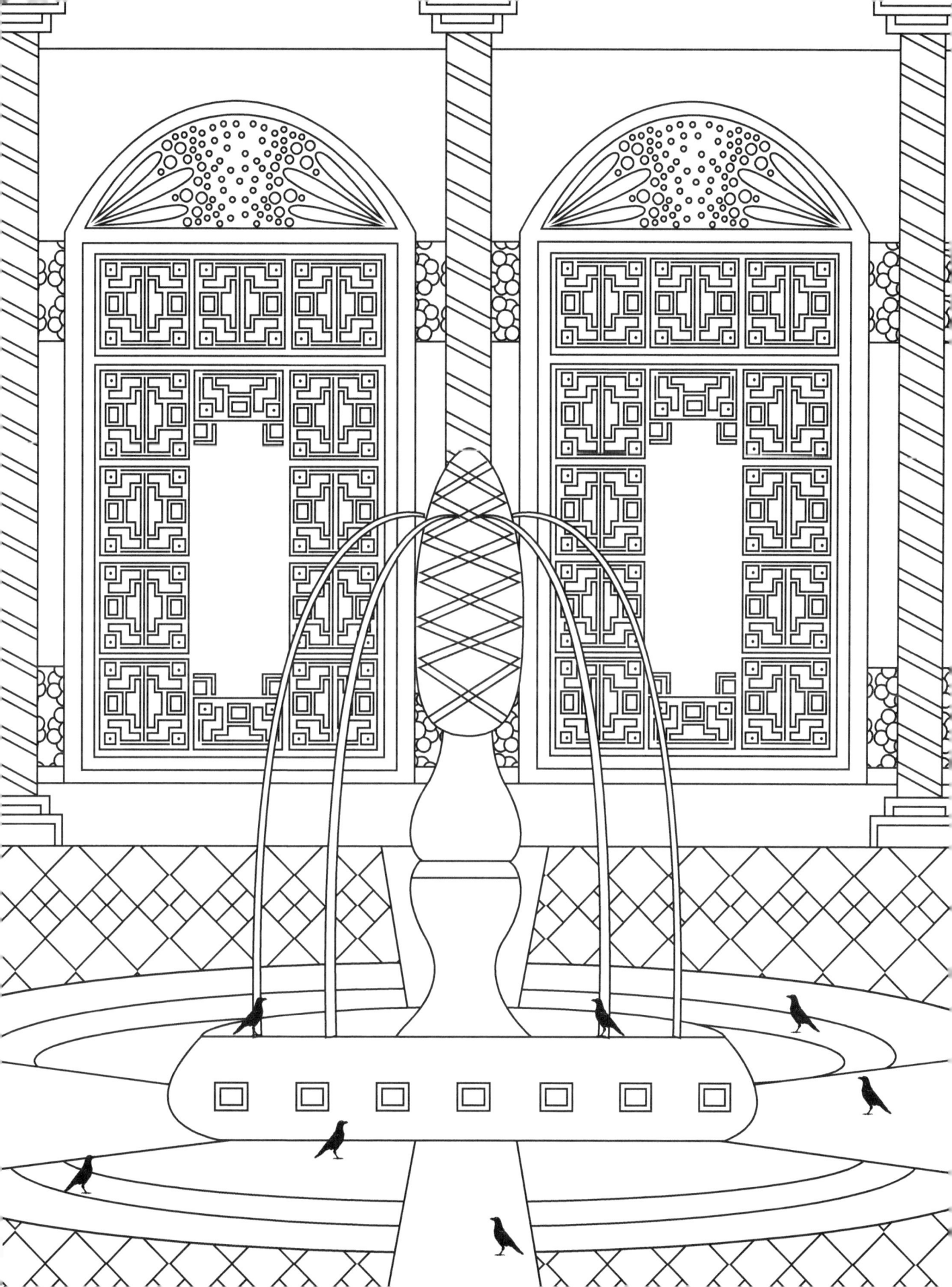

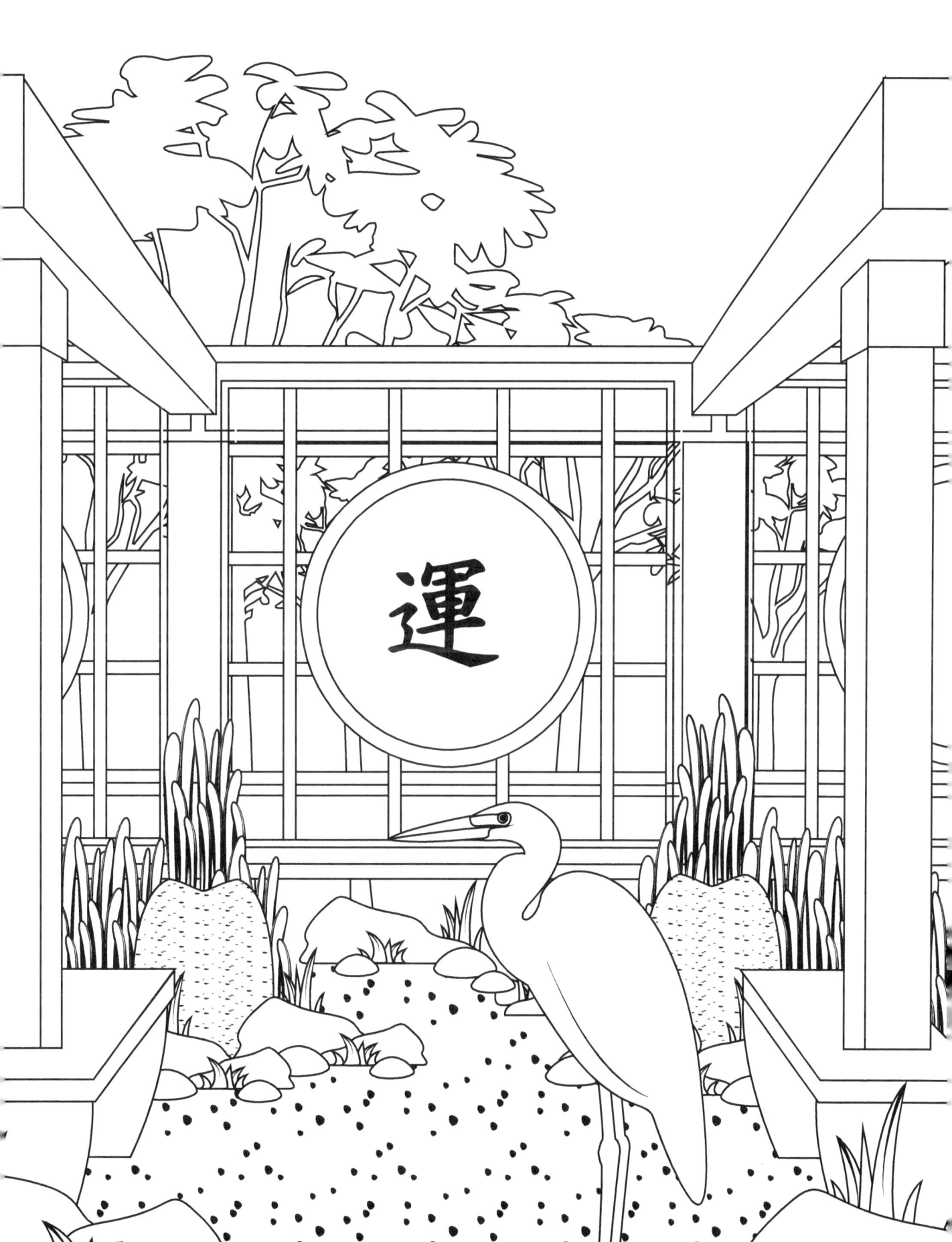

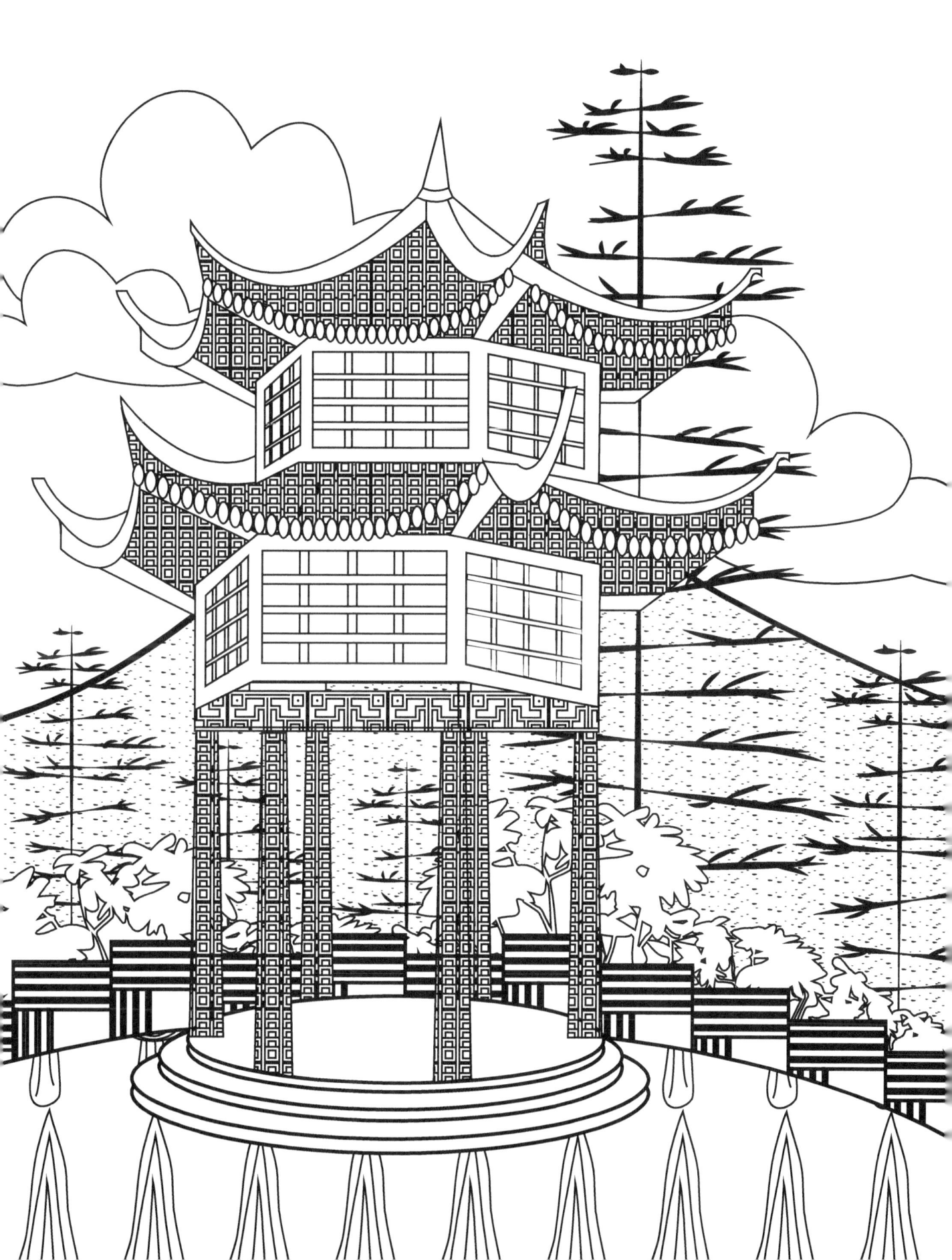

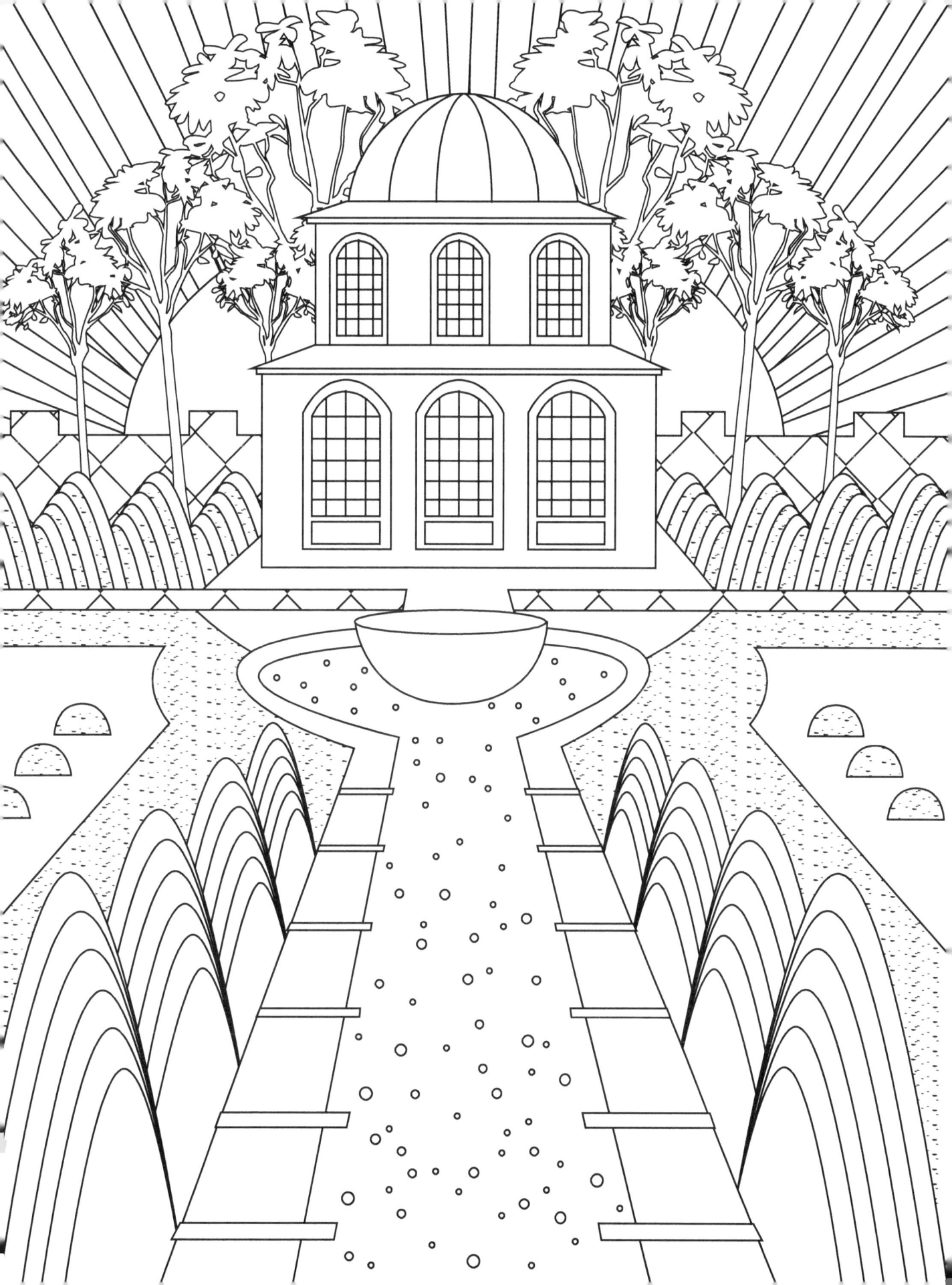

About The Artist

Skye Wright has had a love affair with art since early childhood. Self-taught, she learned through trial and error, study and practice, patience and persistence. As an adult, she added in an eclectic education of work, travel and college to make her the artist she is today.

Birds Eye View is her follow-up coloring book to Faces of Culture.

You can find more products by the artist by going to her website.

www.skyewright.com

or

shopping at her online store
www.etsy.com/shop/weezwompdesigns

www.ingramcontent.com/pod-product-compliance
Lightning Source LLC
Chambersburg PA
CBHW062231220526
45471CB00009B/3437